CW00707941

WILD NEW ZEALAND
A JOURNAL

PHOTOGRAPHY BY
ROB BROWN

CRAIG
POTTON
PUBLISHING

To my darling Mum
on her 80ᵗ birthday.

Enjoy your stay in NZ
& record your thoughts
& travels in this lovely journal

lots of love

Paul

xx

Photography © Rob Brown

Cover photo: Lake Mackenzie, Routeburn Track, Fiordland National Park

ISBN 1-877333-25-5

Published in 2004 by Craig Potton Publishing,
Box 555, Nelson, New Zealand. Email: info@cpp.co.nz
www.craigpotton.co.nz

Printed in China by Everbest Printing Co Ltd

Foreword.

The gift of such a beautiful book with wonderful photographs needs some justification to be used simply as a logbook of events and thoughts.

My being here at all at this time has its immediate origins some five weeks before Christmas when my husband, Noel, died suddenly of pneumonia following a fall at home.

David, my elder son, insisted that I must not be alone at home at Christmas. Instead I joined his family for the festive season, which proved to be much more enjoyable than I had ever expected to be possible.

Then Paul, my younger son, said the 80th birthday is a special one. He and David agreed that I must not be alone for that. Then, since I had Christmas with David, I must have that special birthday with Paul.

So here I am back in Auckland, where I spent my honeymoon, and loving my return to New Zealand.

Anne Kershaw.

25·2·2006.

Monday 20th February.

About 2.5pm I felt worried about the weight of my luggage. I went and took out both swimsuits, a whole group of tops and some light jackets — which I later regretted.

I had just put out the old flowers and the bags of rubbish into the bin & begun to put the pots of plants onto a water-feeder with one end in the bowl when Lilian and Barbara arrived. While they put my things in their car, I went over to say "goodbye" and "Thank you" to Roy and Laura. By 3.15pm. we were on our way to Manchester Airport — a much bigger pleasanter place than the old Ringway. We had a very easy run over the M6 and M56 so Lilian dropped me off at the main departure entrance at 3⁵⁰pm.

What a long tedious wait it seemed to be before the Emirates staff opened the lines and the queue began to move towards the reception desk. Once I had my boarding card and my case was on its way to the baggage handlers, I ought to have reminded the assistant that I had warned the airline that I would need help in negotiating those long, long corridors to the gate for boarding the plane. But I forgot! and so did they. Which didn't matter while I had a trolley to lean on and push my things into the main hall with its tempting array of shops.

Eventually having had hot chocolate and a cake while watching all the fascinating activities on the ground below, my flight was called to the gate. Then without the help of a trolley to lean on and carry my things I had a very great struggle to negotiate the seemingly ever-lasting corridors. By the time I reached the entrance to the plane I felt exhausted and was glad to collapse into my window seat.

The plane arrived at Dubai at 4:40am. and then had to move my watch on to the local time of 7:40am. Thankfully a porter took me - and my things - in a wheelchair for the connecting flight to Singapore. The flight from Manchester to Dubai was 3515 miles and had taken 6½ hours.

The connecting plane for Singapore left Dubai at 9:00am local time and reached Singapore after a very easy & comfortable flight. My watch then said 9¹⁵ so I had to move it on to 11¹⁵ pm. local time.

A porter wheeled me through all the formalities to the entrance where a mini-coach was waiting for me and another passenger for the Golden Landmark Hotel. I was given a very comfortable, clean room but even so this hotel should not have been used for tourist travellers. There was tea, coffee & sugar ready to make yourself a drink — but no milk. I was told "you must buy your own" — at nearly midnight? in a strange town? Not very helpful or practical. Nor was there a lounge where drinks could be bought and enjoyed among other travellers. Hardly a good start.

Mt Taranaki, Egmont National Park

Mount Cook buttercups, North Huxley Valley, Ohau Conservation Area

Wednesday, 22nd. February.

After breakfast I discovered that the Golden Landmark has no courtesy shuttle bus/car to Orchard Rd., nor one to the Chinese Shopping Mall.

So I set out, map in hand, to walk to St. Andrew's Cathedral. It seemed further than I thought so I stopped at the National Library and had iced coffee & chocolate cake to give me a rest on the way. It was worth the effort: the Cathedral is as lovely as I remembered it — simple, quiet and with a deep feeling of utter reverence.

From there I tried to catch a 174 bus to the Botanic Gardens, but must have misunderstood the instructions for finding the busstop. So I doubled back towards City Hall. On the way I called in at Robinsons for a plain white or cream longsleeved blouse to act as a cool jacket. No luck – but I found with coral & pink in the flowers which more or less matched with the coral trousers I was wearing.

I went into the CityHall complex and asked how to reach the trains. I was not told, but taken & shown and even helped to find how to buy my ticket to the Chinese Gardens. Noel and I had so much enjoyed our day there during his 80th birthday celebrations I wanted to enjoy it again. But I soon realised that I'd bitten off more than I could chew: gave up at the bridge leading to the Japanese Gardens and turned back. The warden kindly stopped me, brought out a chair and a bottle of water & persuaded me (very easily) to rest before starting on the long walk up the steady slope back to the train station.

I went to the "Ladies" and then to join the train. One of the men in the rail uniform asked if I felt all right & then decided to come with me in the train to make sure I was O.K. He told me I'ld do better to go on one further stop to be nearer to the Golden Landmark. Then he phoned ahead so that when we got out of the train, a colleague was waiting with a wheelchair. They took me up the ESCALATOR! and on through the station. One of them turned back to continue his duties while the other took me right to the Food Hall below the Raffles Hospital opposite the Golden Landmark. All my protests that this was too much were cheerfully overruled & I was very grateful. When I asked for the names of each of them so that I could write in my thanks,

I was given a form (which could equally well have carried complaints.) and I was glad to have it with its ready-printed address for sending in.

After I'd enjoyed lamb chops with green beans and chips I went on to the hotel. There was a man booking some outing at a table near the Reception Counter, so I borrowed a chair and waited until he'd finished. Then I booked a 2 hour cruise round the harbour in a junk the next morning; $23 seemed very reasonable.

Back in my room I was delighted when David phoned — and very glad I hadn't got into the bath.

Thursday 23rd. February.

I was very glad I woke well before the 6^{30}am alarm I'd set, so I was able to enjoy a bath and pack before going to breakfast at 7^{30}am. When I phoned Reception to ask for my case to be taken down, I was told "just leave it outside your room" — when I set out to return my key it had already gone! It was already in the porters' care so that I could reclaim it when I returned for my transport to Changi Airport.

The coach for the harbour cruise had several other places to pick up passengers. It was amazing how much of the city seems to be one huge building site — new roads and new buildings going on every--where.

Surprisingly the junk

seemed to have amazingly few of us passengers — less than twenty. It was a lovely run with a very welcome cool breeze. We stopped at one of the islands and all the passengers went ashore for a half hour to enjoy the park-like setting and Chinese buildings.

On our return we had coffee and biscuits. A Philipino lady joined me and we enjoyed quite a long chat as we set off round the rest of the harbour and back. It really is huge — there were dozens of large cargo and passenger ships in sight everywhere. Apparently a big ship docks there every five minutes throughout the year. It must be one of the busiest in the world.

By the time we returned to Clifford Pier, most people were going off in search of lunch. There was a Chinese shop just near the bus stop & taxi ranks and I couldn't resist a look in. Of course I found the beautiful silk goods not only pretty but promising to be cool to wear. I bought two short sleeved blouses, one green and one blue as well as a black kaftan with lovely flowers on both back and front. Then I added a lovely red kimono as a very attractive dressing gown. And then they added a shawl for me. I hadn't really intended to shop for so much on the way out but it's so hot I think I'll be glad of the cool silks in New Zealand too.

I was so far from the hotel — and the coach had taken such a meandering route — I was glad to get into a taxi to go again to the Food Hall at the Raffles Hospital.

I wandered round the food outlets and chose one of the Chinese dishes. But it was served with a big ball of rice on a separate plate and several side dishes. It was very tasty but far too much of it. I shared a table with a Bhuddist lady who was most interesting. We agreed on the folly of religious wars & that we're all climbing up the same mountain by different paths in search of the one God whose name only seems different because we speak in so many different languages.

Eventually I crossed the road and returned to the hotel to wait for my transport to Changi. Once there my case was soon on it's way and a porter had a wheel chair for me. We stopped in the duty free area, but I didn't want to buy anything except a coffee and

West Ruggedy Beach, Rakiura National Park, Stewart Island

Goblin forest, Cone Ridge, Tararua Forest Park

a strawberry tart. I asked the porter to join me as I didn't like eating there on my own while he had nothing; but we chatted at least. Then he took me to the right gate and waited ages until he could take me into the lounge ready to move forward.

Then he asked me to sit in one of the lounge chairs — and he and my wheelchair disappeared. No problem until others were brought in wheelchairs & left in them. Panic stations! Eventually I told the porter with the gentleman in the wheelchair next to me that I didn't know what had happened. He soon found out and someone else came with a wheelchair for me, and at last we all boarded the plane.

Friday 24th February.

What a long journey it seemed to Brisbane! And sorting out the time & altering my watch again made me check that it really was Friday.

Again I was very thankful for the use of a wheelchair through all the formalities of customs and baggage checks; though I did wonder what they imagined could have changed in moving from one plane ready for the next.

There was a very long wait. The connecting plane was very late but eventually we boarded for the final leg of the journey to Auckland. It was a gloriously sunny day & there was Paul — lovely to see him at last, dressed in real summer togs of shorts & top trying not to look too astonished at my arrival in a wheelchair. But as I said to him — as I had to each porter in turn — I can walk short distances quite well. It's the long, long corridors that defeat me.

It was quite an experience to join the crawl over the new motorway bridge from the city to Devonport and Paul's lovely bungalow. Ella didn't seem very sure of me at first but soon decided I must be harmless after Paul and I took her "walkies" in the local park.

How good it was to return and sit in the garden enjoying both the sunshine and the flowers. Paul was surprised I wasn't more tired; but I'd had a good sleep on the plane.

When I was making notes of the day's events Paul decided to give me my

80th birthday present a day early — this beautiful book and a delightful card. I shall certainly enjoy and treasure it.

Before going to bed I had the pleasure of a long relaxing soak in a bubble bath! Gorgeous!

Saturday 25th February.

After a good night's sleep I thoroughly enjoyed sitting out in the garden for a breakfast treat of bacon and eggs with homegrown delicious tomatoes.

Later we went down into Devonport where I bought postcards, calendar and a strip of pig magnets. Ella was so good, waiting patiently in the car having a snooze while we shopped.

I was easily persuaded to lie down after lunch & amazingly I slept so long that Paul had to waken me ten minutes before the Skybity car was to pick us up. I really hadn't understood what a wonderful evening was ahead. At Skybity we left the car and joined one of four

beautiful & comfortable coaches. Paul
introduced me to several people as
we went along & everyone was most
kind and welcoming.

When we reached the Park &
left the coaches to stroll over the grass to
join the crowd I felt even more grateful
to Paul for arranging for me to have my usual
Saturday morning 'shampoo & set' — I would
have been so embarrassed to let him down
at such an event with my hair looking an
absolute mess.

I was most fortunate that
Paul took me into the VIP enclosure
for a preconcert meal of salmon,
prawns, stuffed chicken roll with green
beans & a baked potato (thank goodness
it was a small one!) with a helping
of rice and a brown bread roll.

A lovely Thai girl thought —

Ridge above Lake Ronald, Fiordland National Park

Bells Falls, Egmont National Park

correctly - that I was feeling the wind a bit chilly & wrapped a beautiful warm stole round my shoulders. She insisted I should keep it round me although she must have felt the wind cold too.

After we had finished the meal a slight sprinkling of rain made Paul re-organise the seating so that more of us (including me) moved right within the tent for shelter in case the rain developed.

The Symphony in the Park had a wonderful programme. Not only classical music but music from shows like South Pacific as well as contemporary modern music. Even if you were far from the stage everything was in clear view as a huge TV screen had been set up, o the music was also relayed directly to the tent.

Then in the interval we favoured few in the VIP tent were served strawberries with cream & ice-cream, to say nothing of wine and coffee. Superb.

The two TV presenters who hosted the show thanked SkyCity and all the other businesses that had supported the show. All the proceeds from the production are to go to Variety - the charity which provides specialist wheelchairs & other aids needed by handicapped and/or deprived children.

Then after more singing and dancing & other music there was an impressive display of lazer beams and sheets of green light. The band of the Royal NZ Army had brought a cannon with them to give an authentic rendition of the 1812 overture. And when the canon sounded the fireworks began! It was a wonderful display As the finale to close the show we all stood to sing the New Zealand national anthem; & sing "Happy Birthday" to Sky City who celebrated 10 years in Auckland.

The people at the same table with me did me the honour of lifting their glasses to me for my 80th birthday too. It was a wonderful night.

Lilian phoned to wish me a Happy Birthday too — unfortunately she rang in the middle of the national anthem; but Paul managed to phone her back for me once we returned home. And David phoned too.

Sunday 26th February.

After such a wonderful and exciting late night, it's not at all surprising that I slept late. At 8am when I went to the bathroom Ella left her "Duckie" on the bed and went to cuddle up to Paul.

We had break then took Ella down to the beach before going into Devonport for coffee and a walk round the shops — quite a lot of them were open.

Then back home to the garden to enjoy the sunshine and relax in a really lazy day, with plenty of leaflets to study from the tourist information centre.

Monday 27th February.

Paul made a lovely selection of fresh fruit for breakfast.

We took Ella along to the Park but didn't stay long because a boisterous – but gorgeous – huge dalmation–cross puppy bowled her over and frightened her.

Back in the car we went to Devonport and I was able to cash a traveller's cheque at the bank and buy stamps and postcards to send back to England & Scotland.

The wind was chill and I was glad of my fleece. We thoroughly enjoyed taking the ferry (after we'd taken Ella home) over to Auckland city. It's a much smaller, very much more comfortable

comfortable one than the old one I remember from 1951. It travelled much more quickly too and we were soon across the harbour. At least the two Terminals are still the same.

It was a delightful walk round to the Chinese restaurant where Paul had made reservations. We had a lovely welcome from the assistants there and were soon shown to a lovely window table. Tea was quickly brought, soon followed by tempting baskets of shrimps, scallops wrapped in bamboo leaves and shrimps with vegetables. Absolutely delicious. While Paul joined the queue to pay for our feast I slipped across to say how much I'd enjoyed it. Then Paul found it was 'for free' as my birthday present! Wonderful.

Rata forest, Enderby Island, Auckland Islands

Te Whaiti Nui-a-toi Canyon, Whirinaki Forest Park

Tuesday 28th February –

Slept late again this morning and Paul did too as he'd been to a friend's last night with some mutual friends from Australia.

It's raining so Paul's lending me a light mac in case we go out. He's busy on phone & computer sorting out the possibilities of our travelling to the north tomorrow.

Well the rain's stopped and the sun's shining so Paul's spent quite some time getting us booked so we really are taking Ella up north with us tomorrow.

We took Ella with us and went into Devonport for me to buy stamps & post envelope to Prizes Galore – it should be there well before 12th March. Paul bought me a gorgeous box of handmade chocolates — a really extravagant treat I'll enjoy. It turned into quite a shopping expedition: I got a pair of batteries to use in my camera while the present ones are recharged in the fantastically quick charger I bought the other day: my ordinary batteries can't be used in it. Then I bought a new tin of talc and (was I extravagant? I don't care!) a super pair of sunglasses for $79·95. We saw some beautiful candles & I wanted to buy a set of three for Paul — but he'd have only one tall one. So we sat in the sun & enjoyed "flat whites" in cups that might serve as soup bowls.

It was a lovely sunny afternoon quietly reading in the garden. Paul cooked a super dinner — steak with pumpkin, potatoes & carrots. So good we didn't sample the chocolates until later; they were truly worth waiting for!

Wednesday 1st March.

What a wonderful day - fine &
brilliantly sunny. Paul loaded up the
car with everything we might need &
set off on a glorious run along the
M1 motorway northwards. We stopped for
morning coffee at the Kauri Museum, where
I also bought a teatowel and a paua
thimble.

As we came close to the
turn-off for Waipu I asked Paul if we
might call there & he quickly
agreed. It was lovely to be back
tho the little village has grown into
quite a big town. There is a Heritage
Site there now with all kinds of
souvenirs & tapes available. I couldn't
resist the one entitled 'Waipu'
telling the story I know so well of
how the Rev. Norman Mcleod brought
the ships from Scotland, to Canada &

on to Australia before landing & settling in Waipu. I was so happy here it's good to see it's now even better with cave beaches & other sights even more well-known than ever. I took quite a few photos before we left.

Once we reached Whangarei I asked if we might visit the waterfall. We walked only to the top of it & were very worried as Ella made a dash for the pool above it and jumped in! I thought Paul was going to have to go in after her to rescue her — the side was steep & she couldn't get out. But Paul rescued her in the middle of an important business call — but all was well & she's safe.

We continued on through hilly forested roads with glimpses of the sea we came to the Braeburn Resort Motel on the Tutukaka Coast, halting en route to take photos at the Lookout Point. We could a wonderful panorama of sea, coast, hills and beaches in every direction but behind us. I'm so glad Paul was willing to bring me; and that he's not been here before and is enjoying it.

The chalet we're using is a delight — I could happily LIVE in it! There's a walk-through living/dining and kitchen area with two bedrooms and a bathroom. It's spacious and well equipped & even has a top fan which will spin at various speeds. What more can you ask?

Paul took Ella and the car and went for a swim while I had a snooze. I wished I'd gone to the beach with them — I could have slept ~~and~~ on a towel & I'd have been so very much cooler. When they came back, Paul phoned a friend & checked the best place to go for a meal.

We went to the Yacht Club
at Tutukaka. It was lovely sitting
out by the marina. I had some
delicious fish with chips & salad. But
there was so much fish Paul had to
help me with it. It was suddenly
dark & really chill so we went
"home" about 8:30pm.

An absolutely superb day.

Thursday 2nd. March.

What a wonderful day. It had rained early on o there was a hint of drizzle in the air but we were showered and repacked before 9am. Ella had been such a good dog — she slept in the car with no fuss and no grumbles.

The machine was reluctant to take my Visacard for the $120 over night, but eventually settled for $100 and I gave a $20 note as well — at least it worked in the end! We had lots of help with notes on an extra map o we were away — but poor Paul forgot he'd left his floppies on the verandah o by the time he remembered he said we'd come too far to go back for them.

This coast road is fantastic — always going either up or down and quickly curving right and left giving wonderful views over valleys & gorges alternating with bays and beaches.

We stopped for breakfast at a tiny settlement as we re-joined the main road - unusual perhaps but welcome & delicious hot steak & mushroom pie straight from the oven. Then a few miles on to stop for 'flat white' coffees.

Signposting is not always clear; so once we followed the road to Whangaruru, going past oysterbeds which made Paul drool as we pushed on. We stopped at a little store & 'enjoyed' the poorest coffee we've had but I took the opportunity to photograph a huge rock I've christened 'The Tower Rock' because it looked like a Norman tower or round keep plonked right on the top of the huge cliff. Still we pushed on, the road becoming narrower and rougher round each bend as we said 'This can't be right!' And it wasn't —

Mt Sefton, Westland/Tai Poutini National Park

Sawcut Gorge, Isolation Hill Scenic Reserve, Marlborough

we literally ran out of road and had only just enough room to turn on a little space with sea lapping on three sides of us.

Back we went having enjoyed the diversion. At the junction where we'd misread the signs, we looked long and hard trying to sort out whether we should now turn left or right. Fortunately a car pulled up beside us and a girl jumped out and put us on the right road.

Eventually we went through Kawakawa to Paihia for the car ferry to Russell in the Bay of Islands. It's a lovely big tourist centre (it even had a bank so I was able to change another £100 travellers cheques) I'd wanted to take the cruise to the Hole in the Rock - but finding it was a four hour trip, I sadly said 'tough luck' and after another coffee buying a few post

cards and a new pill box for me we set
off back to the ferry. Straight on board
and away to Puketona & on through
Kerikeri, Waipapa and Kaeo to Mangonui and
along the southern edge of Cable Bay. At Awanui
we turned north for Pukenui where Paul had
reserved us a Tourist cabin.

When I'd looked at the map I'd said
to Paul that north from Awanui the road
looked like a return to the twisty
turning roads like the one to Tutukaka.
And it was! It's a good job that Paul
is not only a good driver but enjoys
it as much as I do.

The Tourist cabin at Puketona
was quite basic, but clean and comfortable
with a block of showers, loos & laundry
available. No complaints, No it was a good
job Paul had brought bedding with us. A couple
from Cornwall joined us for dinner in lovely modern
restaurant. Another wonderful day.

Friday 3rd. March.

What a wonderful day – the early morning shower soon passed although the way the clouds are rolling towards us, there'll be more.

After a lovely breakfast of bread & butter with honey & banana it didn't take long to pack up all our things. Paul soon stowed them in the car, stripped the beds of all the linen & duvets Paul had brought & they too were packed in the car.

In spite of the uncertain forecast we decided we were so close to Cape Reinga we really must make the journey & we were away by 9.30 am. For most of the way there was a superb sealed surface. When we reached a signpost to turn right for 3 km. to the Cape, the surface changed to very rough gravel – in fact it felt as though a tank had pressed deep caterpillar tracks in to it before the lower level had had the gravel dumped over it. The road climbed & twisted for more like 13km. giving us wonderful glimpses of many delightful bays.

We never saw where we had expected to have to leave the car and join a coach for the last lap. Just before we reached the Cape itself we pulled off the road to photograph a huge bay and watch the waters of the Pacific & Indian Oceans smash against each other and rise up to then race up to the beach. It was an amazing sight. The couple from Cornwall pulled up their campervan behind us & we agreed to go on as far as we could. In a very short time indeed we were there at the Cape itself with the lighthouse just a short walk away.

The bus, coaches, campervans and cars made a changing kaleidoscope of vehicles as people parked and wondered at the tremendous strength of the wind and the beauty of the surroundings. No wonder the Maoris have the legend that on death one's spirit travels through the earth here to the sea and on to eternity.

We soon said goodbye to our Cornish friends as Paul had to face the return journey in frequent heavy showers. How lucky we had been to have such a lovely fine break here.

Once back at Houhora we had coffee at the tavern where we'd had such a lovely meal last night. As we got back into the car, the heavens opened again & the rain lashed down. Was it worth going along to see the NinetyMile Beach? A break in the rain & return of the sunshine made us decide to go for it.

The narrow good road soon changed to gravel & we went on admiring the variety of trees crowding in on both sides. When we reached the sandy end of the track Paul got out & went to look. I was glad I'd stayed in the car — down came the rain again. Paul dashed back and we soon began to retrace our way back to the main road.

We soon came to another turn-off for NinetyMile Beach, now in sunshine & on a very good road. Part of the forest on either side of the road had been replanted not only with native trees but Australian gums and some fir trees for later logging. This time we reached the shelter of the dunes to park and went on the beach right to the water's edge. Wonderful. And the wind was so strong I could hardly stand.

Delighted to have seen both the Cape and the Beach we returned to the main road watching for wild horses said to live in the forest. We didn't see any but Paul saw a grouse!

Once we reached Awanui, we turned south through Kaitaia on the Twin Coasts Route. It was very different country — wild gorges sometimes giving way to gentler agricultural land. We had a rest-stop by a river in

Broadbank to eat a late lunch, then went on in search of somewhere for coffee.

Unfortunately we found a lovely café & enjoy flatwhites & chocolate cakes not knowing that just round the bend the ferry we needed was leaving for Rowena. A very frustrating wait for it's return and our crossing.

Finding somewhere to stay overnight became urgent, but third-time-lucky Paul secured the most beautiful cabin in a lovely motel. There was a good restaurant & bistro and we enjoyed our burghers on the very sheltered patio.

As Pepys said - 'and so to bed' after a wonderful, marvellous day.

Kauri forest, Waitakere Ranges Regional Park

Archway Islands, Wharariki Beach, Golden Bay

Saturday, 4th March.

This Opononi Tourist Hotel is absolutely 1st Class — two beautiful bedrooms, kitchen, shower & toilet unit as well as a beautiful big living room with a balcony through the sliding doors. And Opononi is absolutely right on the water's edge. I'm sorry we can't stay another day.

After a breakfast of bread, butter, honey and banana we repacked our gear and Paul stowed it in the car before we went down to the Office to settle the account — very reasonable & no problem with my Visa card this time. There was a lovely navy blue Opononi top with a dolphin logo on display. When I tried it on it was a perfect fit so Paul bought it for me : yet one more lovely gift to make an extra happy memory for future years.

We set off through Oponini but digressed up to Lookout Point. There was wonderful surf on the sea side and a sheltered bay on the lea. But the wind! Again I was nearly blown over.

Back on the main road for Dargaville we drove along very twisty twining bends through greens of every shade in the forest. At first there were not many kauri trees to be seen. Paul pulled in at the stopping-place to walk to the oldest kauri tree left in the country. The whole atmosphere of the forest leading to it was wonderfully still and reverent. Paul made me look away through the forest until he had guided me to where the tree was in the middle of a group of native trees surrounded by a protective wooden fence. It is so huge towering up over everything else it is absolutely awesome! I just sat there in wonderment -- how could our Victorian ancestors be so greedy and enjoy such wanton destruction as to almost wipe out these ancient beautiful trees. At least now there's some protection and some re-planting. Eventually we quietly made our way back to the car and set out again towards Dargaville.

It was wonderful to travel along the narrow forest road with the native trees now including some young-ish Kauri trees. We saw a directive to a fresh-water lake some 11 km. away and we enjoyed the run to see people sailing yachts and also water-skiing behind speed boats. We didn't linger long but returned to the road to Dargaville.

For mile after mile we ran through the wonderful forest. Then it began to alternate with cleared land now used for farming with lovely views of the sea & its bays and mountain tops in the distance.

Dargaville town itself was a disappointment, but the Museum was well worth the journey. Not only did it have artefacts from the old way of life but it had a reconstruction showing how the Kauri gum was dug up, cleansed and used. Most went to the USA with the most of the rest going to England.

Before we left the town we had a late lunch of a panini and a sandwich; both lovely and we had half each with a cup of coffee.

We joined the M14 for Whangarei and soon went through it to the Egyptian Lodge at Rawera to see Paul's two horses. One is a yearling and the other a two year old. They are beautiful. Foalcon, the two-year-old was friendly enough to let me stroke his nose.

Soon we left and continued our way towards Auckland with lovely ever changing views as we travelled. It was amazing how much lovely countryside is within the city area.

As we came into Devonport we stopped at the clifftop fields for Ella to enjoy a free run around. She was happy to be home too and gambolled like a young puppy. It has been a wonderful Northern trip, but so good to be safely home. She has been

such a really good dog she deserved
that treat. Right from the first night
at Tutukaka where she was not allowed
in the chalet she had to sleep in the
car – but then she decided that that
was good and went to sleep in the
car each night.

Paul made us a light meal
of paté & tomato on toast with champagne
in beautiful flutes. To complete the
celebration of a happy journey and
a safe return we sampled more of
the handmade chocolates.

I felt as tired as though I had
shared the driving so Paul must be
exhausted. I was delighted to have a
long luxurious bubble-bath and, again
as Pepys said, 'and so to bed'.

Sunday 5th March.

What a quiet restful morning!
We took Ella to run in the park and
drove down to collect the Sunday paper
which we read in the garden after
breakfast.

Paul did a lot of chores – loads
of laundry – but I fell asleep in the
livingroom. When the strong wind crashed
one of the doors I awoke to find Paul
talking to David!

After a sandwich lunch we went
into Devonport & had coffee at "Ice It" and
then went up into Victoria Park. I took photos
of Rangitoto, the motorway bridge (which I
think is probably too poor) and Skylike
Tower. Then we had a run round some
of the streets with particularly lovely
houses. On returning home I didn't need
much persuasion to go have a nap.

While I slept, Paul prepared a gorgeous chicken curry with pumpkin, peas, carrots and rice. Where does he get the energy? He did all the driving on our tour & I'm tired enough as a mere passenger? But oh, it has been so lovely. I hate to admit it — but I don't want to go home next Sunday.

Ever since two inches was taken off my bladder before the radium treatment for cancer, I have needed frequent comfort stops. But after that lovely meal I was horrified to discover I'd 'leaked'. When I put on fresh briefs and slacks & took the others to be washed Paul was wonderful: he didn't allow me to be embarrassed — simply said "It happens as you get older".

Fresh snow, Haast Pass, Mount Aspiring National Park

Clinton River, Milford Track, Fiordland National Park

Monday 6th March.

A lovely sunny morning
quite a bit calmer. We took Ella
for her walk after breakfast and then
went on into Devonport.

I walked up the hill to find
the good bookshop Paul recommended —
everything but banks and coffeeshops
was closed. Paul had been unlucky
too: his hairdresser wasn't in today.
I went into the candle shop to see
if they had any almond ones
left — only two, one small and
one medium so I was able to
complete the set for Paul. He says
he uses a lot of them in the
winter so I'm especially glad
they still had those two left.

All the shops nearer to the
waterfront seemed to be open and

I tried on several hats; they were O.K. but there wasn't one that absolutely shouted "Buy me" so I went on in to a bookshop. There were plenty of books on fish, birds, fjords and everything else but N.Z. trees. But I found a lovely copy of "Auckland is a Garden" which at least was full of beautiful flowers

As I was paying for my book, Paul came with a beautiful gardening book - not only flowers but trees too. He bought it for me so I was thrilled to bits. I'll love studying that at home.

I called at the Bank to change another £100 travellers cheque before we brought Ella home as we're not taking her with us into Auckland. Paul said last week that we'd make Monday my shopping day — he wasn't kidding! I'd said I need a lightweight navy jacket for now and the summer at home, so it was the first thing we looked for. On the stand near the jackets was a display of woollen throws which could be arranged like a stole or a poncho or whatever — irresistable! So we carried a lovely decorated black one while we searched for a navy jacket. Soon found one — perfect.

So on to look for gifts. Vera had a paua shell ring which is broken so I bought her a new one and a navy top. A similar top for Lilian and a pillbox with a paua-shell top. Then I added a green top for me with a NZ "map" on it and a letter opener. Great. So then, what for David? Paul spotted some lovely heavy tops with an easy collar-zip — great for sailing or a cool day walking.

Paul has booked one o'clock lunch for us at a superb Chinese restaurant called SUNSHINE. The girls brought round trolleys of food in covered wooden baskets. We had prawns with veg. and coriander in balls, then fish similarly both with soy sauce and chilli. Then NZ. duck with plum sauce followed by mango custard with cream. It was all delicious.

Back on the ferry I took photos of another ferry and the Hilton Hotel both managing to give the impression of ships. When we reached the shore we had to stand with the car doors open to try to make the car cool enough to get in — then windows right down helped to cool it more.

Then home to sit in the cool shadows in the garden reading todays papers, before having a "roastie". Paul put a wonderfully clever penguin on the computer to write Anne Kershaw. Wonderful day.

Tuesday 7th. March.

A pleasant quiet start to the day. Breakfast in sunshine in the garden browsing over the morning papers.

Took the batteries out of my camera & put them into the fantastic new NZ charger — they were fully charged in ten minutes. Must get some more comparable batteries to take home, and check the right adaptor plug I'll need.

We went down into Devonport for coffee with Pete Lawrence and his wife Karen. It was a delightful social occasion; they are charming. On the way back to the car I bought ½ metre of grey material which will, I hope, make the trunk of a Kauri tree (with a great deal to spare) for only $1.50. Incredibly cheap. While I was buying that Paul went shopping for salmon for tonight's dinner: he really is an excellent cook.

This afternoon Paul took me through Takapuna and on to Brown's Bay. It began to rain so that it was hard to tell where the sea ended & the rain clouds began. The scenery was beautiful. The peninsular is so narrow in places that as we turned one bend the sea was on the left, turn another and the sea was on the right. Quite fantastic.

Paul took me on to see the industrial estate. It is so big & so well set out if you can't find something you want there, you'll just never find it.

We went along quite a few main routes and then Paul said he knew a place I'd love and he took me to SPOTLIGHT. It was fantastic. As I went in I saw a notice to go upstairs to find bins of remnants and cheap material by the metre just as Paul said I would. It was irresistible. I asked the assistant how small a run I could buy — 10cm. So taking a piece from one of the bins with several colours I wanted, I started to look through the big rolls for as many different greens as I could. Paul soon joined me & suggested not only that I should take the other similar piece from the bin but also look for some navy blue to use as a cushion backing. I had a lovely selection of material for only $28. When

We went downstairs again, Paul said he knew another area where I'd love the things on display – he was right. I bought two balls of edged ribbon which should help to make leaves and/or ferns and also two ½metre lengths of light material with pretty designs. I really am going to have to set to work to use them well when I return home.

It was a delightful way to spend a rainy afternoon.

After Paul's lovely dinner of salmon, scallops with salad, we watched the news, the Antiques Road Show and Paul's DVD of Wallace & Grommit and The Curse of the WereRabbit. It was fun and so cosy in candlelight.

The First Day Cover – I posted to Paul on 7-2-06 arrived today. A full month later!

Sunrise, Papakiakuta Ridge, Ruahine Forest Park

Lake Mackenzie, Routeburn Track, Fiordland National Park

Wednesday 5th March.

The Races — The Auckland Cup today. It's dull, but at least the rain is holding off so far.

We had a leisurely breakfast (indoors) over the morning papers then Paul took me to the hairdresser's for my 10:30 am appointment. They did it beautifully — well worth the $37. Paul was sitting waiting for me by the entrance then we were away to catch the 11:45 am ferry across to Auckland city.

The wind was so fiercely strong that I walked down through the shopping mall to try to keep my hair tidy while Paul parked the car then caught up along the outside walk to the ferry gangway. We stayed in the lounge this time and watched (and felt) the choppy waves.

Once we reached the shelter

of the inner harbour the sea calmed down & we made an easy landing. Once on shore Paul saw one of his Skycity assistants waiting to chauffeur us through the city to join the coach in front of the Skycity building. Several of the people there remembered me from the Symphony in the Park concert & greeted me as Paul's Mum. They were very welcoming.

As we travelled over the motorway to Ellerslie Paul gave me a tie-pin type of button to put on my top, a lanyard to hang round my neck with the entrance card to the VIP lounge and a green entrance ticket to the racecourse itself.

By the time we left the coach the threat of rain seemed to be over and it was becoming a beautiful, sunny day. We went up to the sumptuous VIP room to be greeted with a choice of champagne or orange juice and canapes as we were told the number of our table. Paul and I were favoured: we were at Table 2 right at the front of the room by the windows overlooking the course itself. There were ten at our table, two ladies were people I'd sat with at the concert, they made me so welcome it was lovely. As people came to speak with Paul I was introduced as 'Paul's Mum from England' and everyone wanted to know that I'm enjoying my visit. It was lovely to see how well-liked and respected Paul is; although he was officially on holiday he was soon up greeting people and making sure everything was O.K.

Other people at the table were from the Seychelles and the Philipines as well as the Auckland people I already knew. All of them were so friendly I never felt left out of the fun or the conversation.

The meal was a gourmet lunch of soft shell crab with chilli and tomato, mini eye fillet of beef, wrapped in dry cured bacon, scallop mornay with lime and chives, Chinese crispy duck breast with soy & oyster sauce, saffron rice and a selection of salads. Ours was the first table to be invited to come and help ourselves to this wonderful selection of food beautifully cooked and served.

While we were enjoying the meal, the racing began. From time to time people left their tables to go and place their bets while we at the tables could watch the races & other happenings on the course from large television screens. There were extra seats all along in front of the windows and glass doors open to tiers of seating outside the stand so people could go out and watch a race wherever and whenever they wished.

Later in the afternoon the desserts were arranged along tables leading to coffee and Tea. Like the main course, the desserts were lovely with a selection of Kapiti cheeses with crackers and dried fruit too. Quite irresistable.

Everyone had a race card (really a little booklet) and a pen on their napkin at each table, so it wasn't long before I, too, was choosing a likely winner & placing their bets. Fortunately before setting out I remembered Uncle Teray's advice — never take more than you're willing to smile about if you lose. So I had put all my money I was going to keep into the back of my wallet out of temptation. Although I lost more than I won, I enjoyed my flutter and the excitement of the horses reaching the winning post

right in front of me. I told Paul
how Grandma Cheyne had dreamed
winners (my Grandma, his great
grandma). He was astonished as,
he said, he has dreamt them
too : not often, but they have won.

It was amazing how quickly
the time fled past. The last race
was at 6³⁰pm. and by seven we were
moving back to the coaches. Judith had
stopped me when returning from the ladies
rest room. D told me to take the lovely
arrangement of flowers on the table
home with me. I said I wasn't sure
if Paul would want me to do that,
but eventually I did anyway.

Back at Skybily, there was a car
waiting for us again, but instead of taking
us for the ferry, we were soon home after
another wonderful day. But Paul is a
long way from his car.

Thursday 9th March.

A lovely sunny start again. Paul said he was taking Ella for a walk & he gave her a good long one — down to Devonport to collect his car.

Now after breakfast we're packing a bag between us so we can stay overnight in Coromandel if we wish. Paul had hoped to be away by 11:00am — but we were away by 10:00.

We crossed the motorway bridge & across Auckland remarkably easily and on to the Southern Highway, & continued south along the M1 until we reached the junction with 2 east for the Coromandel peninsular. The views were absolutely fantastic with excellent sealed roads except for places where road repair or maintainance was in progress.

At Tairua Paul spotted a bakery so we stopped for coffee and a pie each, then shared an apple cake before driving to the water's edge and back.

It was wonderful climbing through native forest then out with a view across farms to the mountain tops and the sea in quick succession.

When we reached Hot Water Beach I was glad to take off my sandals to walk in the hot sand. But when I wriggled my toes deeper into the sand it was even hotter from the volcanic action below. We drove further along and saw people who had dug into the sand and

Rainforest, Milford Track, Fiordland National Park

Winter snowfall, Pleasant Range, Fiordland National Park

allowed the hot water to fill the holes where they wallowed in the warmth. Amazing.

On again past Cooks Beach to Hahei where we found a fair-sized settlement. We had coffee & cakes and I bought some little forks with paua shell on the handles. Paul went to a big camp area but we saw "No Dogs" as we went in around the roundabout and straight out again. Then he tried the one near the café — not as nice as some we've been in, and $200. No thanks.

So on to Whitianga. It's a much bigger township than I had expected with a lovely harbour and plenty of boats. The very first tourist centre we tried had a vacancy & a lovely two-bedroom cabin with the usual living-room, kitchen and bathroom with separate shower & toilet. Fantastic — $80. Better than $200! And the weather continues gloriously sunny.

About 7pm. we went into the township and had a long, slow delightful meal at The SALT restaurant and by nearly 9pm when we returned we were ready for bed.

It was lovely to talk to Paul over that super meal and know that if/when he goes to Macau or somewhere like that, he'll take Ella with him and rent out his bungalow until his return to New Zealand. We talked of so many things it was a very precious interlude.

Friday 10th March.

How strange it is: I've never even thought about my silver charm bracelet until I woke this morning. With all the charms from so many places how is it I've not added a fern from New Zealand or a boomerang from Australia?

After breakfast we went to the photographers I saw in Whitianga township. Paul was very patient waiting while I got new batteries. I also wanted a new memory card to store the photos but the assistant persuaded me to have a CD made and re-use the card when the photos were erased. Bought a manicure set while I was busy too as I'm having a series of broken nails.

We went on to explore a whole series of wonderful coves & beaches. Again we went up along corkscrew bends with views of native forest, logging of farmed pines and agricultural land alternating with the islands, beaches and mountain tops. Fantastic.

In Coromandel town itself we stopped for lunch and coffee — and I added a piece of apple pie before we went "walk about" round the town. We saw a lovely motel and Paul took details & a phone number for a future stay.

We decided not to push on right to the very tip of the peninsular but to cut across country through Thames. That was a much bigger town than I expected and I told Paul it looked like an upmarket Blackpool — which he said was no compliment. He was right — it wasn't!

We continued an interesting twisty, upsdown route until we reached the tremendously long bridge over the wide inlet which can flood so easily and so often. The mudflats are a haven for wild water birds.

Once we passed this section the road suddenly became much straighter with a wide plain of farm land on either side. Vineries and orchards were protected with enormously high windbreak hedges — so high it seemed more sensible to simply call them windbreaks rather than

Ledges.

As we joined the (25) and the motorway ① the road suddenly became so straight and hypnotic we could well understand the warning notices like "Another accident through falling asleep".

Fortunately Paul negotiated the heavy traffic across Auckland & over the bridge very safely if slowly at times. We were very glad to be home shortly after 4⁰⁰pm.

I sat in the garden and took some photos of Paul's lovely flowers & shrubs. He's given me a lovely Sky City bag to carry my books & maps on Sunday. And a lovely bath ended another wonderful day.

Saturday 11th March.

Ella left me when I went to the bathroom at about 2º°am. but she was back at 7ºº_am and cuddled in and licked me. I wonder if she'll miss me? I told her I won't be her cushion in the car after tomorrow — she'll have the front seat all to herself. She just cuddled in!

It's another beautiful sunny morning. Paul took Ella for a walk & to collect milk and the morning papers as usual. Then we a cup of tea with toast & ginger marmalade and read the papers until Paul drove us to Takapuna to have breakfast with Ingrid. It was great to see her at last. She's thoroughly enjoying her new job and travels all over. I hope she finds the green leather travel handbag useful; she seemed to like it.

After breakfast & a long chat she went of to keep an appointment while Paul took Ellard me back to the car and down to Devonport.

I wanted to go into the little shopping mall — tourist trap — by the ferry terminal. I bought teatowels (for me & others) coasters and two hanging maps of New Zealand. Paul was very patient as I pottered and then we went up into the township for stamps to post the last of my NZ postcards.

While Paul went across to the bank I wandered into another shop full of tempting trifles & of course bought some. Then I asked Paul again if he'd like me to buy something for his garden. He had seen some white

Mt Owen, Kahurangi National Park

Catlins River, Catlins Forest Park

orchids he'd like, but on the way we passed a fashion rail outside with two tops Paul thought looked nice and should fit me. So I went & tried them on — a navy one & a lovely turquoisy-green one. While I was trying them on Paul gave another stripey blouse/jacket with lovely stripes of plum, brown, grey etc. to the assistant to pass to me. Of course I finished up buying all three.

While I paid for them Paul brought the car up and we went for his orchids — just as they closed! Fortunately they saw us and opened up for us to buy the beautiful pot of white orchids.

Then home to rest and Paul showed me how to look for house types & prices in the Manchester/Cheshire areas. It was extremely interesting but I still need a lot more help in how to use a computer. I really must have lessons organised once I'm home.

In the evening we sat on the front, Paul with a beer & I with a gin and tonic. Then we went to an Italian restaurant (owned by a Greek Paul knew.) We shared a pizza and a cannelloni. The pizza was O.K. but the cannelloni was much better. As the dusk deepened towards 8pm. we started for home. But we stopped to watch a couple feed the ducks and other water birds ——— They did a real "pied piper" following the couple till they went & got more for them from the boot.

Truly another delightful day.

Sunday 12th. March.

At 7:30 am I had an extra
set of instructions 3 options show on
my phone when I tried to speak to
Lilian. Fortunately, Paul was awake
and sorted out what I needed to
do. By the time I got through to Phil
Lilian had left for a meal with
Barbara. Good for her! So I gave her
my good wishes through Phil.

Then I went and looked
at the way my case is piled up
with stuff — and so much still
on hangers or lying on the bed.
Panic Stations! Paul says he's
good at packing! I can see the whole
lot coming out and starting again.

After lunch - it did. Paul
has loaned me the lovely big bag we
shared on our Tours of the Northland

and the boomandel – but oh, it is
so heavy to be taking into the plane's
cabin.

We took Ella, now again in
lovely sunshine like a good summer
day in England and went down into
Devonport for coffee & cake. While Paul
had a second coffee I went across to
the shop where I bought the butter and
cheese knives & matching fork yesterday.
I bought a different pair of matching
dainty knife & fork as a gift.

Then we wandered down to
the waterfront & called in at the library
on the way. I was astonished it was
open from 09^{00} – 16^{00} on a Sunday.
We sat on a bench by the beach and
watched the boats for a while and then
began to make our way back to the car.

Ella had very sensibly

settled down in the shadow in front of the forward passenger seat and was fast asleep. She soon scrambled on to the back seat and we were soon home.

Paul put all my gear into the boot & we set off for the long drive to the Airport. I'm sure Ella knows that I'm leaving — she made much more fuss of me than ever before.

Once at the beautiful airport (how it puts Manchester to shame!) Paul found where the Emirates were boarding. They had already begun, so Paul & I had to say goodbye. I'm glad he didn't linger and see me cry but I couldn't help it.

At the booking in desk I put my case on the ramp, but the girl asked me to put the cabin case on to be weighed. Too heavy for the cabin. So I had to put one of their luggage labels on and hope for the best.

Then I was sent to the service desk to fill in my departure form and wait for a porter with a wheelchair for me.

The girl who took me through the halls & up the lifts to the boarding gate was from SALFORD! We had quite a chat on our journey. I was taken first on board & shown to my seat. Fine — until three people came and said I must be in the wrong seat, I was — an otherwise empty plane & I was put on the wrong side of the gangway i soon remedied.

We had dinner en route for Brisbane & then a long wait there to change for the next plane to Singapore.

At first there was no one else with me in the row of four central seats and I began to think of Paul's advice to lie across them all and go to sleep. But a young Arab lady came and took the farthest one, so I tried to make myself comfortable on the next seat as well as mine. She saw what I was doing & asked if I felt ill. When I said I was just tired she helped me stretch out across three & covered me with the extra blankets.

When I woke the others were having dinner and we were well over Mount Isa & nearing Katherine. I had a glass of iced water & felt much better.

Later on I returned the favour & helped her to get comfortable & sleep until we were nearing Singapore. We were very prompt in arriving at 00.55 on Monday "morning". Again a porter with a wheelchair was waiting for me & I was quickly whizzed through all the formalities and was soon waiting anxiously at the carousel for my case and bag. I was most relieved to see them on their way & the porter grabbed them for me. He had asked a colleague to fetch a trolley and then we were straight through immigration and customs & out to the big hall.

There was a driver waiting holding up my name to take me to the Mirimar Hotel. Unfortunately he had to pick up another passenger as well. We waited until 02.10 & when he still hadn't arrived the driver eventually took my luggage round while I got into the car. After the long drive from Changi Airport it was three in the morning when at last I checked in & went to my room.

Coastline, Paparoa National Park

Earland Falls, Routeburn Track, Fiordland National Park

Monday 13th. March.

What a lovely hotel the Mirimar is — very attractive as well as comfortable and well equipped. I needed a drink of tea before falling into bed & the porter said just ring room service and milk would be brought for me. It came very quickly and I was thankful to enjoy it before getting into a very comfortable bed.

I had set my alarm for 8⁰⁰am. but I was awake and up before it rang, and had a cup of coffee & then washed and dressed. Last night before I fell into bed I was so glad they gave me soap, toothbrush and toothpaste so I didn't need to find my spongebag.

After breakfast I went to the Tours desk & said I wanted to go and ride the cable car, paid for my ticket &

agreed to meet the tour bus at 1³⁰pm. Then I joined the shuttle bus to Orchard Road. One of the first shops I found in the Paragon shopping mall was travel supplies. I soon found luggage labels and little padlocks but also spotted canvas holdalls like Paul's but smaller. After hovering a bit I bought all three items & went looking for somewhere to buy a little silver Merlion to put on my bracelet. I couldn't find one so was extravagant and bought one in white gold.

Then I looked for a camera shop & was delighted to put a bigger memory card into my camera. I missed the shuttle bus back to the Miramar so I took a taxi which cost only S$5.

I enjoyed an Indonesian dish for lunch & signed for it before I went to the tour bus. It was not as I

asked just a journey to enjoy the
cable car but a whole series of events
on Santosa Island. We were to meet
up together again at 5^{15} pm. and I was
glad of the idea of returning to the
hotel — but no, after sitting & resting
a while we were to meet again
at 6^{30} pm. to go ready to see/hear the
musical fountain.

What a walk! Fortunately
there was a series of escalators
between sections. The hillside was
a huge series of terraces of
beautiful flowers. When we at
last reached an amphitheatre in
front of waterfalls flowing into a
pool with fountains playing I was
thankful there was an arena of
seating facing it.

There was a very long wait
while thousands of people eventually

took their places and the display began.

There was a series of coloured jets rising to different heights and making a variety of patterns. I took a lot of photos, but I don't have high hopes of any of them being any good.

I was delighted when the guide collected us together to walk a much easier route to the coach park which must have held well over 60 large coaches.

We were back at the Mirimar at last at 9.30 pm. and I was exhausted & glad to make a drink of tea and go straight to bed.

Tuesday 14th March.

As usual I was up about 2¹⁵ am. but went quickly back to sleep.

Got up about 7³⁰ am and begun to pack. Put warm beige trousers, my "tiger" top and cardigan as well as my mackintosh and green fleece all into the new canvas bag to go with me into the cabin — I hope.

Went down & had breakfast, paid the bill for my extras and then rang & asked the "bell" room for help with my luggage which they soon took down for me to put in store until tonight.

The receptionist was very kind when I went to change some $NZ into S$ and told me that there's a hospitality suite on floor 5 where I can rest or have a shower etc. at any time until I leave.

I took the shuttlebus to Chinatown but I couldn't find the walkover bridge lined with Chinese stalls with the fantastic range of oriental things like fans & embroidered tablecloths & napkins I remembered. However I did see some lovely craft shops where people were busy making some lovely ceramics.

Then I passed a jewellers with a display which included several things I would have liked to have, but guessed they'd be beyond my pocket. One sales girl came to ask if there was anything I'd like to see. Of course there was! A beautiful black brooch in the shape of a flower with diamonds set on one petal. I guessed it — over £300. Another lovely black pendant — a long bow with diamonds set against each end. I should have guessed —

even more than the first. Then there was a piece which could have been a brooch or a pendant. It was a set of silver or white gold curves linked and set with pearls; really lovely. Eventually I was persuaded to try it on; and of course I really loved it. I've no silver or white gold chains, so of course it needed one to look perfect. And of course in the end I bought both --- I just couldn't resist. So I spent over £135 on an exquisite piece of good jewelry I'll always treasure.

When I left the shopping mall I went along the shops & "eateries" most shops were Chinese. There was a bargain box full of small items including tiny teapots. I bought a white one with a lovely blue design on it. I looked for four dainty little cups to go with it, but couldn't find any.

Before I went to wait for the

shuttle-bus back to the Mirima, I realised I had time for a drink so I went into the welcome coolness of "Aunty Kate's" and had iced café-latté : very refreshing.

The shuttlebus arrived very promptly & I was soon back at the Mirima for lunch. After lunch I took the shuttle bus again; First I made arrangements for my luggage to be stored until evening, then I went back to the Pargon shopping mall. and had a snack ~~tea~~ and an iced caffé-latté — very refreshing. Afterwards, I took a taxi to the Raffles Hotel. I wandered round the main entrance & studied some of the bars & what they said about them, and took several photographs. One couple took my camera and "snapped" me at the edge of the fountain within the Raffles complex. Then I went in and had afternoon tea — the menu was so large I wondered if one had to choose from each section : but

Key Summit, Routeburn Track, Fiordland National Park

Mountain beech forest, Arthur's Pass National Park

no it would all be served on a three-tier silver cake stand; two scones on the top tier, about eight cakes on the second and thin finger-strip sandwiches on the base. The waiter reassured me that there was no need to eat it all at once — he would pack anything from it I wished to take with me!

He took a photo of me before I started to add cream & jam to one of the scones, and eventually packed the cakes & sandwiches in the fanciest "doggie-bag" I've ever seen. But the contents made a very welcome supper in the evening while waiting for the taxi to come to the Mirimar for me.

Amazingly the taxi arrived more than half an hour early and the porters had to rush to collect my luggage & take it out to the taxi.

The ride to Changi Airport seemed even longer than the ride from it to the city. Again the porters were very willing to help. The Emirates desk had already opened, so I was soon in a wheelchair being taken for the long wait to board the plane. On the way the porter stopped at the Duty Free mall and I bought a 1.14 litre of St. Remy brandy and 1 litre of Johnny Walker Red Label.

Eventually I went on board with a couple of other people in wheel chairs. The stewardess put up my canvas bag & duty free bag into the overhead lockers. Then when everyone else was on board, we set off.

Wednesday 15th March.

It was an easy flight to Dubai, but it seemed strange that time was apparently going backwards as we travelled west.

The food on board was mostly pretty good and enough of it so that you could leave what you didn't care for and still not be hungry.

Once in Dubai there was a rush through the formalities and then a long journey through corridors over the shopping mall. I was very glad I didn't have to walk.

By the time we reached Gate 36 we joined a group of seven others in wheel chairs. We sat by the open door watching other passengers cross to buses to take them to the plane.

Eventually we were wheeled to an uplifted, boxlike contraption into which each of us was put by a hydraulic lift to put us in our wheelchairs & safely carried right to the entrance of the plane. Quite extraordinary — very efficient.

From there we continued in daylight — beautiful sunshine — all the way to Manchester. The only fly in the ointment came at the carousel in Manchester when my canvas bag arrived safely but no case. The porter helping me said it would probably come on the next flight. The girl at the baggage desk promised to phone at 7^{30} p.m. and tell me if it had arrived. Bless her, she did and it came home at 10^{00} that night.

When the case arrived, I could hardly believe my eyes. All the locks had sprung open and the lid was some inches adrift & held in place only by the strong strap right around it and through the handle. It was a sorry sight with everything bunched up right away from the handle. I feared the worst — but amazingly nothing seems to be missing.

What an extraordinary way to end such a wonderful journey. It has been a delight of dear people, fantastic sunny weather almost the whole time, wonderful exciting experiences travelling in this beautiful country giving me a treasure-chest of lovely memories.

Yet the journey itself did not end at Manchester Airport. There Lilian and Barbara had waited hours not knowing what had happened. But after a lovely welcome they too had reassured me that there was nothing to worry about; both of them had

had luggage lost & always found. So they took me home to complete one of the happiest journeys I have ever made.